3/07

From Past to Present

A History of Cars

by David Corbett

GARETH STEVENS
GS
PUBLISHING
A Member of the WRC Media Family of Companies

Please visit our web site at: www.garethstevens.com
For a free color catalog describing Gareth Stevens Publishing's list of high-quality
books and multimedia programs, call 1-800-542-2595 (USA) or 1-800-387-3178 (Canada).
Gareth Stevens Publishing's fax: (414) 332-3567.

Library of Congress Cataloging-in-Publication Data

Corbett, David, 1937-
    A history of cars / David Corbett.—North American ed.
        p. cm. — (From past to present)
    Includes index.
    ISBN 0-8368-6286-4 (lib. bdg.)
    1. Automobiles—History—Juvenile literature. I. Title. 2. Series.
  TL147.C668   2006
  629.222'09—dc22   2005054080

This North American edition first published in 2006 by
Gareth Stevens Publishing
A Member of the WRC Media Family of Companies
330 West Olive Street, Suite 100
Milwaukee, WI 53212 USA

This edition copyright © 2006 by Gareth Stevens, Inc. Original edition copyright © 2003 by ticktock Entertainment Ltd.,
First published in Great Britain in 1997 by ticktock Media Ltd., Unit 2, Orchard Business Centre, North Farm Road,
Tunbridge Wells, Kent, TN2 3XF. Additional end matter copyright 2006 by Gareth Stevens, Inc.

Gareth Stevens editor: Leifa Butrick
Gareth Stevens designer: Kami M. Strunsee

The publishers would like to thank Graham Rich, Hazel Poole, Rosalind Beckman, and Elizabeth Wiggans for their
assistance, and Annice Collett, Roger Bateman, and the picture research staff at the National Motor Museum.

Picture credits:
t=top, b=bottom, c=center, l=left, r=right
All pictures supplied by the National Motor Museum, Beaulieu, except: Ann Ronan@Image Select; 26l. Mary Evans Picture
Library; 4l, 20br. Nicky Wright/National Motor Museum; 15tr, 30cr (Citroen), 31tr.

Printed in the United States of America

1 2 3 4 5 6 7 8 9 10 09 08 07 06

CONTENTS

Words that appear in the glossary are printed in
boldface type the first time they occur in the text.

No achievement has changed our lives as much as the invention of automobiles. Whether we love them or hate them, automobiles are the most successful form of transportation, and, for most people, they have become an essential part of daily life. The story behind the development of automobiles is long and interesting. In 1335, Guido da Vigevano drew up some plans for a sail-driven vehicle, although we have no evidence that he built one. By the late eighteenth century, steam seemed to be an obvious source of power, and some unusual-looking, steam-driven vehicles appeared. In 1803, Englishman Richard Trevithick invented a steam-driven car that could carry eight passengers and travel 12 miles (19 kilometers) per hour. One night, however, he left his car in a shed next to an inn without putting out the fire the car used to make steam. Both the car and the shed burned — just one reason that inventors started to look for another source of power.

Imagine That!

Born in 1452, Italian painter and inventor Leonardo da Vinci created designs for vehicles that were very much like our modern submarine, helicopter, and automobile. There is no proof that he ever made a horseless carriage, but a model does exist. It was a tricycle with a gear on the rear wheels that allowed the outside wheel to turn faster on a corner than the inside wheel. This model was, in itself, a remarkable invention.

First Try

The first vehicle to move under its own power was invented by Frenchman Nicholas Cugnot in 1769. It was a steam-powered tricycle with a huge **boiler** in front of a single front wheel. Steering was very difficult because of the weight on the single wheel. On its first time out, it knocked down a wall! With a top speed of 2 miles (3 km) per hour, it was never a success, and no one built more. A reconstruction of this machine can be seen at the Conservatoire des Arts et Métiers in Paris.

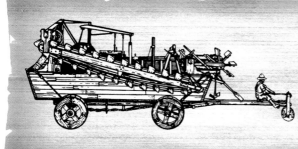

Is It a Duck?

The first recorded horseless carriage in the United States was a boat on wheels, with a steam engine that propelled it on both land and water. It was built by Oliver Evans in 1804 and was called Orukter Amphibolos.

Reinvented Invention

R. W. Thompson's invention of rubber tires was an interesting accomplishment. He made the tires for horse-drawn carriages (*below*). Thompson also patented the first **pneumatic tire** in 1845. It had a leather covering with several tubes inside. Thompson's invention was unknown to William Dunlop when he "reinvented" the pneumatic tire for bicycles in 1888.

Things That Go Bump in the Night

This early nineteenth-century cartoon (*above*) makes fun of the idea of a steam-driven vehicle. In England, a man named William Murdoch made a similar machine, using a small steam engine attached to a child's tricycle. While he was trying it out one night, it got away from him and terrified the local minister.

The Steam Coach

The first auto passenger service was the James' Steam Coach, invented by John Scott Russell in 1829. Disaster struck, however, on July 29, 1834. A wheel on the steam coach collapsed, the boiler exploded, and five passengers were killed. This accident was just what the opponents of road vehicles wanted. Most of them had investments in the up-and-coming railroads, and they managed to have laws passed and road tolls increased, severely restricting the development of automobiles for many years.

The first cars powered by **internal combustion engines** did not use gasoline for fuel. Instead, they used a mixture of coal, coal gas, and air. In 1860, a Belgian named Lenoir designed the first coal gas engine. A spark made the gas in a large **cylinder** explode, and the explosion drove a **piston** that turned a crank, which moved the wheels. Austrian Siegfried Markus developed engines that ran on gasoline. In 1864, he mounted an engine in a small handcart, making the first ever gasoline-driven car. Markus lost interest in building more, however, and left making and selling new cars to others. Many people had a hand in the development of the automobile, but two Germans stand out — Gottlieb Daimler and Karl Benz. Although these men worked separately, they were the first to build and sell automobiles to the public.

The Hot Tube Ignition Engine

Automobile engines were comparatively simple at first, and **water jackets** to cool the engines were a part of them from early on. **Valves** allowed a mixture of gasoline and air to flow into a cylinder and let exhaust gases escape. An internal explosion moved the piston that turned the wheels. The timing was haphazard, and the explosion sometimes took place when the exhaust valve was open — an event that prompted the title of the film *Chitty, Chitty, BANG! BANG!*

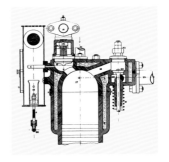

The 1884 Benz

Karl Benz (1844–1929) came from a poor family but started on the road to success when he built his first motor tricycle. The public was suspicious of his "driving machine" and thought it was powered by secretive devilish forces.

One morning his wife, Bertha, stole the vehicle and took their two sons on a 62-mile (100-km) trip. When the news spread that a woman and two children could make such a trip safely in a hissing, snarling, horseless carriage, the critics were won over, and the Benz started to sell.

Early Advertising

Karl Benz took his car to the Paris Exhibition in 1887. He used an agent, Emile Roger, to sell his cars in France, and so the automobile industry was born. Advertising was used to attract customers, a tactic that has continued to this day.

Daimler and Maybach

Gottlieb Daimler (1834–1900) made gas engines for the company of Otto and Langan. With his friend, Wilhelm Maybach, he produced the Otto Silent Gas Engine, which is acknowledged as the world's first **four-stroke engine**. He left Otto and Langan when he was forty-eight years old and, along with Maybach, moved to Cannstatt, Germany. There, they produced a small, lightweight engine that ran on liquid fuel. Daimler bought a second-hand carriage and installed one of these engines in it.

The 1898 Cannstatt Daimler

The Cannstatt looked like a **brougham** carriage without the horses. It has been said that Daimler was an old fuddy-duddy to have produced such an old-fashioned car. The design of the car, however, worked well. It was easy to drive, and the four-horsepower engine produced a maximum speed of about 16 miles (26 km) per hour. After Daimler's death, the Cannstatt was developed into the first Mercedes.

Emile Levassor

Emile Levassor (1843–1897) had seen a Daimler car for the first time at the Paris Exhibition of 1889. He didn't like the car itself but was intrigued by its engine. Daimler had given his attorney a license to build the engine. When the attorney died, the license became the property of the attorney's attractive widow. Levassor, who had been a friend of the attorney, fell in love with the widow and married her. Under French law, the license to build Daimler's engine then became his. In his first car, Levassor put the engine in the middle, under the passenger seat. Later, he placed it at the front of the car, which became the traditional layout of car design.

Germany took the lead in developing automobiles, and auto races had a great effect. The first races took place on ordinary roads between large towns. Companies such as De Dion-Bouton, based just outside Paris, gained popularity by winning races, which were followed avidly by the press. Companies in Great Britain suffered because restrictive laws set the top speeds for cars at 4 miles (6 km) per hour in the country and 2 miles (3 km) per hour in towns. Early cars had no uniformity in design. Without horses, cars could be steered in a variety of ways. Some firms used a wheel. Others copied the tiller of a boat or the handlebars of a bicycle. Using the skills of the existing workforce, many automakers copied the bodywork of carriages for their automobiles. Wooden bodies and leather seats were popular. Cars at this time were still "playthings of the rich."

Outspoken Critics

In the early days of automobiles, relationships between drivers and the rest of the population were strained. Some people said cars would ruin crops with the dust they produced. Others claimed car exhaust was poisonous and said cars would kill people and animals when they went out of control. Much of the protest was orchestrated by people, such as horse breeders and railroad investors, who realized that cars could make dents in their incomes.

Beep!

Drivers used various devices to warn people of their approach. The most common was a horn like this one (*right*), which was a bugle with a rubber bulb.

Driving by Candlelight

The first headlights were candles and gave little light. They were usually set in a long tube that contained a spring to push the candle up as it burned down. Later, oil lamps (*left*) were used for headlights, as on the 1903 De Dion (*opposite*).

Going Forward by Going Backward

Many early cars had small engines. This De Dion engine (*right*) is typical. It had no gasoline pump, so gasoline was fed from the car's gas tank by gravity. For the most part, this method worked well, but, when the car went up a steep hill, the gas tank was lower than the engine, and the gasoline stopped flowing. To continue, the car had to be turned around and driven up the hill in reverse.

The Crank

Early drivers had to turn a crank to start a car. Even with a small engine, this task was difficult and dangerous. Many people broke their arms as a result of poor technique, which is one reason women seldom drove cars in those days.

Changing Gears

Every make of car had its own way of changing gears. The De Dion had a lever on the left side of the steering column. Drivers pulled the lever back for first gear and pushed it forward for second gear. Reverse gear was engaged by pressing down on a pedal with the right heel. The **accelerator** lever on some cars (*right*) was on the right side of the steering column.

1903 De Dion

This car (*left*) is an example of a typical early twentieth-century automobile. Drivers had little or no protection from the weather, so most drivers took their cars out only during the summer. The wheels were made of wood, and the tires were pneumatic, replacing the solid rubber tires of the late Victorian period. Pneumatic tires meant frequent stops to repair flats, which were caused mainly by horseshoe nails on the roads.

When larger cars came along, drivers demanded more luxury, and cars became status symbols. The rich employed chauffeurs to drive their cars. The chauffeurs wore uniforms that signified their employers' status. Cars were exported to countries such as India, where the local maharajah rode in an exotic car that displayed a level of luxury befitting his station in life. To an automaker, royal patronage was a distinct advantage. The Daimler company let everyone know that the Prince of Wales, who later became King Edward VII of England, bought one of its cars. Protection from the weather grew more important as the use of the car gradually changed from a rich person's plaything to a useful part of everyday life. Open cars gave way to cars with **hoods** and then to cars with enclosed passenger seats.

The Ultimate in Luxury

The interior of a car's passenger compartment could be built to the owner's specifications. Many were copies of first-class railroad carriages. Some even had speaking tubes so that passengers could give instructions to the chauffeur. The interiors of automobiles were now often opulent, with velvet upholstery and blinds on the windows. Quite often, cars had protective railings on top to hold personal luggage when families went on vacations. Usually, servants and most of the luggage would precede a family on a trip to make sure everything was ready when the family arrived.

Elegant Headgear

Catalogs advertised special clothes for driving for both men and women. Women's hats needed to be securely fastened with a scarf or several hat pins, and veils in front kept out the dust that rose in clouds from the dry summer roads. In winter, men wore heavy coats, some with detachable leather linings, to keep out the cold. Women had large foot warmers filled with hot water.

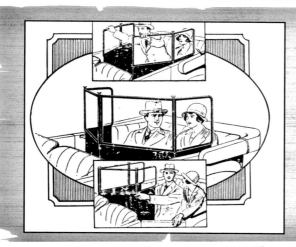

Early Windshields
Folding **windshields** became popular on open-top cars so that passengers could wear fashionable hats. These windshields often were built into the front of the back seat and could be unfolded quickly when needed.

Family Fun
Going on a picnic became a popular way to spend the day. Wealthy families wore their elegant city clothes, even at beaches. If it rained, they climbed into the enclosed rear compartments of their cars. The chauffeur of the car in the picture (*left*) had a windshield but when it rained, the windshield was fastened to the roof.

Dressing for the Occasion
The motorists seen here (*right*) are wearing clothes typical of 1909. The car has a windshield, but it has no windshield wipers. The windshield has to be removed when it rains for the driver to see the road. A basket (*far right*) holds a parasol in case the Sun comes out.

Until the turn of the twentieth century, commercial garages did not exist. Either the automobile owners or their chauffeurs made car repairs. Flat tires had to be fixed on the road, and, because the wheels did not come off a car, the only way to fix a flat tire was to remove the inner tube and patch the hole. The first automobile garages evolved from bicycle repair shops and from workshops for agricultural repairs. The first gasoline pumps were seen in about 1910. Gasoline was pumped from an underground tank, using a hand pump, into a glass tank where the customer could see it. Then the gasoline was released into the gas tank of the car. Each gas station sold a different brand of gasoline, and billboards on the road leading to the station advertised that brand.

I'm a Little Oil Can

When early drivers bought oil at gas stations, the station hands pumped the oil from big oil drums into small cans that had handy pouring spouts. The cans came in different sizes, depending on how much oil drivers wanted to buy, and the cans usually carried the advertising logos of the oil companies.

Attracting Customers

As more garages appeared, advertising their services became important. Some advertising became an art form of its own.

Fixing a Flat

Flat tires were frequent, even as late as 1908, when this picture (*left*) was taken. A "vulcanizer" made the best patch for a flat tire. A vulcanizer consisted of a metal tank that fastened around the inner tire and held a patch against the hole in the inner tire. A driver then poured a mixture of ethanol and **methanol** into the metal tank and lit it. The resulting fire was just hot enough to weld the rubber patch to the tire.

Garage Interior

Many early cars needed service every 500 miles (800 km), so early garages were busy places. In addition to dealing with cars, garage mechanics repaired bicycles, charged storage batteries for radios, and sold chocolate and cigarettes. Mechanics had to be familiar with several makes of automobiles and be able to manufacture parts whenever possible.

The American Garage

All around the world, gas stations evolved in the same way. Bicycle and machine repair shops became garages that offered automobile owners a number of services. Most service stations supplied air for tires, which lost air quickly. Some even sold their air at so much per tire. Stations also supplied water for **radiators**. Suppliers' names were prominent on both the building and the road nearby.

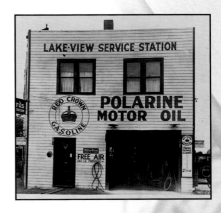

Spark Plugs

The insulation on **spark plugs** wore out often, and wise drivers always carried spares, which they stored in tin boxes or wooden cylinders. The oil systems of early cars were primitive, and, during a journey, a car owner had to clean oily plugs and brush off deposits on the electrodes often.

Gas Cans

Before gas pumps came along, gasoline came in 2-gallon (7.5-liter) cans. The caps on the cans were made of brass because careless use with an iron cap might cause a spark that could lead to an explosion. Caps had turrets on top so they could be opened with levers. Lead seals guaranteed full cans.

Making early automobiles run at all was a battle. By 1907, however, cars became fairly reliable. Daimler's patents on his engines were the basis of Austria's and Great Britain's automobile industries. Count Albert De Dion and his partner, Georges Bouton, also produced magnificent small engines that were light and powerful. Many other companies used Daimler's and De Dion's engines — Darracq, Delage, Peugeot, and Renault in France; Humber in Britain; Adler in Germany; Ceirano in Italy; and Peerless and Pierce Arrow in the United States. These companies went on to produce their own engines and become giants in the automotive world. Eventually, many early companies merged or went bankrupt.

The Mercedes

Austrian businessman Emile Jellinek sold Daimler cars. He persuaded Maybach, Daimler's partner, and Paul, Daimler's son, to produce a brand new car with many new features. Its sides were made of pressed metal instead of wood, its radiator needed half the water, and it used a new, more effective, kind of brakes. The car (*a 1903 model shown right*) was named after Jellinek's daughter Mercedes. Another Daimler car was named after Jellinek's second daughter, Maja, but her name was later dropped in favor of the name of the technical director — Ferdinand Porsche.

The Renault

Louis Renault (1843–1918) had a hard time in school, but he taught himself about engines in his garden shed in France. Like other inventors, Renault bought a De Dion tricycle and converted it to a four-wheeler. He then made a car of his own, using a De Dion engine. Renault was the first person to use propeller shafts instead of chains to drive the wheels. Renault's cars quickly became popular and, with help from his two brothers, the Renault company had a good start. This picture (*left*) shows a 1906 Renault. Its rear compartment is a copy of a first-class railroad car.

The Oldsmobile

Ransom E. Olds (1864–1950) started making steam-driven and gasoline-driven cars with his father in 1895. His 1902 curved-dashboard runabout (*right*) became the first car produced in quantity. Olds had a machine shop where one operation was completed at each bench. His backers wanted to build larger cars, so Olds sold out. William Durant (1861–1947) bought the company. He had also bought out David Dunbar Buick's company. In 1908, Durant created General Motors by adding the firms of Cadillac and Oakland to Buick and Oldsmobile.

The Fiat

The automobile industry in Italy started later than in other European countries. Several small companies in Italy built automobiles, but none of them made a great impression until 1899, when a group of men formed the Fabbrica Italiana Automobili Torino — Fiat for short. Fiat built a small four-seater. The company quickly took off and started exporting to the United States. This Fiat (*left*) ran in the 1912 French Grand Prix.

The Rolls-Royce

One of the most famous automobile partnerships began in 1904 between Charles Rolls (*below*) and Henry Royce (*left*). The two men came from very different backgrounds. Rolls (1871–1910) was well educated and came from a wealthy home; Royce (1863–1933) was poor and had to start working when he was twelve years old. Royce worked as an engineer's apprentice and then started a small firm that made electric cranes. In 1903, he purchased a small French car and set about improving it to his standards. In 1904, he built his first car. Rolls was a race driver who also sold cars in a famous part of London. He was looking for a good English car for his showroom. Rolls liked Royce's car and agreed to sell as many as Royce could produce. In 1906, they built the Silver Ghost, so called because it ran almost silently. This first Rolls-Royce was admired for its reliability and refinement and continued to be produced for nineteen years.

At first, cars were manufactured to order. They were built only when a potential owner ordered one. Cars were built one by one by a number of workers, each with a different skill. This process was costly, and only rich people could afford to buy cars. Ransom Olds was the first person to create an assembly line to produce cars. If his workshop had not burned down, he might not have thought of it. He wanted to produce cars quickly, and when he was rebuilding his workshop in 1901, he came up with the idea of moving the car down a line. Although he didn't realize it at the time, he started a revolution within the automobile industry that drastically reduced the cost of building cars and put the selling price within range of ordinary working people.

The Master of Mass Production

From his boyhood days, Henry Ford (1863–1947) was a master of mechanical logic. He always dreamed of making cars, and, because he had a job as a steam-engine demonstrator, he first thought in terms of steam. When he read about internal combustion engines in English magazines, however, he knew where his future lay. Ford saw a display of Daimler engines at an exhibition in Chicago. He went home and made his own engine out of scrap materials. That was the start of the Ford dream.

1908 — Model T Production Line

Although not the first, Ford's **production line** was the best, mainly due to Ford's meticulous research. He timed every stage and made detailed plans to be sure progress was quick and no one wasted time. A car's body was manufactured on an upper floor and then lowered onto a **chassis**, which was made on a lower floor. Ford more than doubled the wages of his workers, and the cost per car fell until even the workers could afford to buy their own. By 1928, Ford had produced 15 million Model Ts.

The 1920s — No Reason to Hurry a Humber

Like many other automakers, the Humber Motorcar Company started by making bicycles. Later, it made airplane engines, but the company was always renowned for its superbly built cars. Although Humber used a form of mass production, it put quality first, and cost per unit was high.

The 1950s — Mind Your Head

Mass production in the 1950s was still labor intensive, and cars were expensive. Cars in this Renault plant (*right*) moved around the factory floor using aerial railways. Renault went through a difficult period after World War II. Charles de Gaulle nationalized the company, which caused political and union unrest.

The Tin Lizzie

Ford's most successful car, the Model T, came in a variety of forms. It could even be a bus or a tractor. The film industry of the time was quick to see the potential of automobiles and featured many Model Ts. The reason behind the famous expression, "You can have it in any color as long as it's black," was that black paint dried quicker than any other color, which sped up production lines.

Today's Robot Army

The automobile factory of today is nothing like Henry Ford's. Computers are everywhere. **Robotic arms** swoop in as a car passes to spot-weld panels together. Robotic spray guns, controlled by a computer, paint the car using a minimum amount of paint.

The 1920s are sometimes called the Golden Age of Motoring. It was a time of great change, both socially and within the auto industry. Little traffic on the road and few legal restrictions made driving easy. Women experienced a new-found freedom in driving. Some women had driven ambulances and other vehicles during World War I and, with the introduction of electric starters and improved gear boxes, were just as capable of driving as men. Although mass production made prices fall, owning a car still was mainly for the rich and for professionals. The twenties saw the emergence of sports cars, with their large engines and speeds approaching 100 miles (160 km) per hour. Many sports cars used engines that were developed for airplanes during the war. The airplane industry was also the source of inspiration for the first attempts to streamline cars.

The King's Car

The Hispano-Suiza Tulip Wood H6 was of Spanish and French origin. Its engineering qualities were world famous. The **patronage** of King Alfonso XIII of Spain meant that these cars were aimed at the rich and were the continental rivals of Rolls-Royce.

A Car for the Stars

Between the wars, Isotta-Fraschini was the leading maker of luxury cars in Italy. Its cars never quite matched those of Rolls-Royce or Hispano-Suiza but were popular among celebrities in the United States.

Country Roads

Many roads were not built for automobiles originally, but that only added to the excitement. Since few cars were on the road, driving was a pleasant experience. Trips to the country were popular, and picnics were the order of the day.

A New Way to Make Money

Trips to certain tourist spots could result in chaos when it came to parking a car. The seashore was a popular tourist destination, and local landowners realized they could make money by charging people to park on their land. This 1924 photograph of an American beach showed that the automobile trade was really taking off in the United States. Racing cars on beaches became popular in Daytona, Florida.

A Very Fast Car

The son of an Italian artist, Ettore Bugatti (1881–1947) was apprenticed to a Milan machine shop. When he moved to Alsace, France, in 1907, he started to make his own cars, like this Type 43, built in 1927. Bugatti's cars became very successful on racetracks and won many races. The radiators on the front of his cars are shaped like horseshoes because Bugatti loved horses and had stables at his factory.

Women Drivers

A sight rarely seen before — a woman driving a car. Automobile magazines were full of letters from irate men saying that women should stay at home but, for women, driving meant freedom and, from this time on, women took full advantage of their new place in society.

The thirties were the years of the Great Depression. Many automobile companies went bankrupt or were taken over by larger groups. At the same time, automobile manufacturers in Great Britain raced to produce the first car that was affordable for many families. A similar race took place in Germany to produce a "car for the people," or *Volkswagen* in German. Manufacturers made great advances in electrical equipment, **suspension**, and tires during this time. Synchronized **gears** made gear changing easier, but cars still had to have oil heaters placed under them in cold weather because **antifreeze** was not generally available. Cars did not have heaters, and every few thousand miles, they had to be taken to garages to have their valves ground — **decarbonization**. In 1934, Citroën produced the revolutionary **front-wheel drive** but, in doing so, Andre Citroën extended his credit so much that he had money troubles and lost control of his factory.

The Importance of Being Seen

Advertising continued to show prestigious cars in glamorous situations. In this Fiat poster of 1938, (*left*) stylish ladies arrive for an evening out. Advertisers hoped to create the impression that to be seen as successful, people had to have one of their cars.

Puncture Problems

Improvement in tire technology and better road surfaces resulted in fewer flat tires. When one did occur, replacing a wheel was much easier with the introduction of devices such as the built-in **jack**.

IN A CLASS BY ITSELF

Looks Good, but . . .

The beautiful body of the Auburn concealed careless engineering. Errett Cord (1894–1974) took over the company when it was in difficulty and built supercharged cars capable of going 100 miles (160 km) per hour. Some of his automobiles had built-in radios and special compartments for golf clubs.

A Lot of Car

The Delage Motor Company produced cars that both performed well and were beautiful to look at. The styling was streamlined but curvaceous, the forerunner of things to come. The Delahaye company purchased the right to manufacture Delage automobiles in the mid-thirties. Delahaye also made fast motorboats and supplied New York with taxicabs.

The Best You Can Buy

The two Duesenberg brothers Fred (1876–1932) and August (1878–1955), moved to the United States from Germany in 1884. They both loved cars, and Fred became a famous race driver. They produced successful race cars and later branched out into passenger cars like this 1933 model. Their cars were very fast and had several new features, including indicators to let the driver know when to change the engine oil and when to put water in the battery. Several bodywork companies, on both sides of the Atlantic, built truly beautiful bodies for the Duesenberg automobiles.

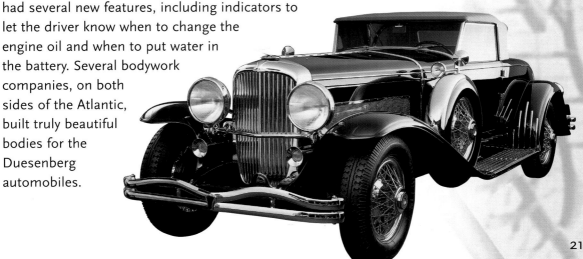

During World War II, car production all over the world came to a standstill. Everything was geared to the war effort. When the war was over, new designs gradually started to appear. The new American cars displayed an abundance of chrome, and their bulbous bodies had fins in back that seemed to increase in size as time went by. Front bench seats and gear sticks on the steering column became popular features. **Running boards and separate mudguards were on the way out. The Volkswagen Beetle, which was first produced at this time, became the most popular car in the world, and other firms started to produce small, economical cars. Firms that didn't change with the times went bankrupt, and many famous names disappeared.**

In a Class of Its Own

Mercedes made a name for itself with cars of excellent quality, strength, durability, performance, and roadholding. Mercedes' racing success left other famous makes of cars lagging behind and boosted its own sales. A horrific crash at Le Mans in 1955, involving a Mercedes 300 SLR, resulted in Daimler-Benz withdrawing from motor racing.

A Very Popular Car

Although very basic, the British Ford Popular was an extremely successful car. The fittings were minimal, which made it 20 percent cheaper than its competitors, but it performed better than some cars with larger engines.

Messenger of the Gods

Several British and American firms used Mercury as their trade name, but the Ford Motor Company made it famous. Its Mercury used a Ford engine but had a longer, lower, and wider body than other Mercurys. This design was the start of "badge engineering" — creating almost identical cars to sell under different names.

Solid as a Tank

In World War II, British Field Marshal Bernard Montgomery used a Humber that was typical of the early 1940s. Big and solid, it was used by senior military officers all over the world. Makes varied according to the country, but the style was the same. Many military cars were **armor plated**, making them very heavy, and they had large engines.

Classy Car

In 1902, Henry Leland (1843–1932) took a redesigned engine to the Henry Ford Company and asked the company to build a car for it. Ford had a disagreement with the financial backers and left, but the company went on to prosper. Leland suggested naming the car after Antoine de la Mothe Cadillac, the French officer who founded the city of Detroit in 1701. Cadillac's family had a **coat of arms** dating from the eleventh century. Used on the Cadillac, it remains the only authentic coat of arms on an American car to this day. The Cadillac Eldorado (*left*) was typical of American cars of the fifties. It had a big engine and lots of chrome.

The Soldier's Workhorse

The first Jeep was built in response to a U.S. government competition in search of a car that was sturdy and reliable, could operate in difficult situations, and could be repaired easily if it did break down. Willys received the contract, but Ford also made the vehicle. In fact, the name *Jeep* came from the Ford designation "G.P.," meaning General Purpose.

Vehicles for commercial use went through great changes in the 1930s. Before then, horse-drawn carts delivered milk and coal, and steam-driven trucks delivered heavy goods. In the 1930s, mass-produced lightweight vans and diesel trucks took over. Buses became standard for sightseeing and cross-country travel, and it was common to see advertising on delivery trucks. In some cases, an ad was confined to a picture and a slogan on the side of the truck. Other ads were more elaborate. Today, commercial vehicles deliver just about everything we buy in stores. We have trucks to deliver gasoline, ready-mixed concrete, furniture, and even nuclear fuel. **Container** trucks now make the transfer of goods to merchant ships an easy job.

Fire! Fire!
The first fire engines were drawn by horses and operated by insurance companies that would put out fires only in houses insured by their own company. Later, models like this 1907 French Gobron Brillie Engine ran on gasoline but relied on a steam pump to provide power for the water jets.

You Can't Squeeze Me
Some vehicles were made exclusively for advertising. This vehicle, shaped like an orange, advertised a brand of South African oranges. It was, in fact, a mini car with a fiberglass top. All the windows except the windshield were orange, which created a warm glow inside the car. It was dangerous to exceed 30 miles (48 km) per hour in this vehicle because a touch of the brakes at this speed might start the orange rolling!

What's the Weather Like Up There?

This Parisian taxi is by no means unusual and probably had its origins in the hansom cab, a horse-drawn cab with the driver in the back. The roof usually had a trap door so that drivers could communicate with the passengers.

All Aboard the 1928 Bus

Because of the great distances between towns, countries such as the United States had extensive bus service. In some ways, bus lines copied the old stagecoach lines, where journeys were so long they had to be completed in several stages over many days. Some early buses were existing cars, such as the Model T Ford, with an extended chassis to accommodate more passengers.

The London Cab

The London taxi is one of the best-loved features on the streets of London. When automobiles started to replace horse-drawn vehicles, taxis transported people around town. Rest huts were built where "cabbies" could put their feet up and have tea.

1907

1950

1997

1999

1907 Some taxis had open storage compartments next to the drivers for luggage. They also had "for hire" arms that indicated if the taxi was available.

1950 Taxis became enclosed with their meters on the inside.

1997 Air-conditioning, pull-down child seats, and facilities for passengers with wheelchairs were new features.

1999 All cab colors are gradually replacing the traditional black cab.

Public roads in France were the first race tracks. Races usually ran between two towns and were governed by strict rules.

The first auto race ran between Paris and Rouen in 1894 and had 102 contestants. No one knows for sure how many cars actually started the race, because most were disqualified for one reason or another. One driver who was allowed to stay in the race promptly drove into his brother's car, then into a cafe, and finally into a ditch, before he withdrew from the race. Remarkably, most of the other contestants finished. The following year, the race went from Paris to Bordeaux and back again. Emile Levassor won, driving forty-eight hours with no relief driver. He was later disqualified for having only two seats in his car — the rule was four seats — but the publicity was good for him, and he sold lots of cars. The first Grand Prix was in 1906 on a 64-mile (103-km) circuit near Le Mans.

Made It!

M. Vachheron (*seated right*) came in fourth in the Paris to Rouen race of 1894. Albert De Dion was the first across the line, but he was disqualified because judges decided that his vehicle was not a car but a steam tractor pulling a passenger coach. His average speed was 11 miles (18 km) per hour.

Hang on Tight!

1906 1ª TARGA FLORIO
Alessandro Cagno in Itala

Besides France, other countries were quick to organize races, and some of the races are still remembered. This photo (*left*) shows a car in the Targa Florio rally in Italy with the mechanic sitting in the side seat and hanging on for dear life. William K. Vanderbilt promoted racing in the United States and was the first American to hold the world land-speed record. He organized the first race on Long Island using public roads. At one point, the drivers had to cross railroad tracks.

Racing Colors

The color of a race car used to indicate the country of its origin. This Lotus (*right*) is the green racing color of England. Now, Grand Prix cars are covered with advertising, which helps pay for racing team costs.

The World's Richest Race

This "Indy" car (*right*) is specially designed for the Indianapolis 500 — a name that means almost the same as "spectacularly fast racing." In 1908, Carl G. Fisher decided that the auto industry in America needed a racing and test track. He bought a farm for $72,000 and built a track that had two long, straight sides and four banked corners. The shape of the track helped the cars go very fast. Thousands of dedicated fans attend this annual race.

Watch Out for the Car!

The Monaco Grand Prix is the only major race still held entirely on ordinary roads. This photograph (*left*) was taken during the 1933 race, a hard-fought contest between Italian rivals Achille Varzi and Tazio Nuvolari (Varzi was the eventual winner). Today's spectators are kept well back from the road, but in the early days, many people were killed because they failed to get out of the way in time.

Today's Heroes

The auto racing driver of today commands very high wages. Racing cars are as safe as possible and built to survive high-speed crashes. Racing clothing protects drivers in the event of a serious fire. Nevertheless, it is a dangerous profession, and many well-known drivers have died or retired because of serious injury.

27

The idea of the horseless carriage has evolved along with the improvements. At first, the concept was just a car without horses. Gradually, people began to think of automobiles as something unique, and they looked for alternative designs. Certain things could not change. A car needed wheels, a chassis strong enough to support the engine, and somewhere for the driver and passengers to sit. New ideas came from existing forms of transportation, and as designers considered people's tastes, they made cars attractive. Changes in technology affected automobile design, and a car's function determined its styling, too. Sports cars need low-weight concentration and widely spaced wheels. Presidential cars need bomb-proof bodies and bullet-proof glass. Family cars need space for weekly shopping.

Go Anywhere, Do Anything

In its various forms, the Landrover drives all over the world. It is not beautiful to look at, even in its upscale forms, but it is supremely practical. Its four-wheel drive allows it to go where other cars dare not go. The aluminum body panels do not rust and can easily be replaced if damaged. The Landrover has many purposes, including fire engine, safari transportation, and farm car.

The Bubble Car

The bubble car, such as the BMW Isetta was a good example of adventurous design. The driver entered through a front door that opened outward. Many models had no reverse gear. This caused problems if drivers parked up against a wall because they had no way to get out. Some bubble cars had only three wheels.

The Car of Its Generation

If ever a car in Britain was a symbol of its time, it was the Mini. Now much copied, this vehicle was brilliantly designed by Alec Issigonis. The Swinging 60s, with its many social changes, cried out for a car that was different. The Mini managed to be a small car that still had lots of space for passengers because its engine was turned sideways to take up less room.

Hood Ornaments

The first **hood ornament** was found on a chariot buried with the Egyptian pharaoh Tutankhamun. The ornament was a Sun-crested falcon, meant to bring good luck.

A jaguar first adorned the Swallow Company's SS Jaguar of 1936. Gordon Crosby designed it, and it was used until 1960. New safety laws prompted the jaguar's removal.

Hispano-Suiza cars were Spanish but built in Spain and France. They used a flying stork in honor of George Guynemer, a popular flying ace of World War I. The stork was the emblem of Guynemer's squadron.

The Spirit of Ecstasy is perhaps the best-known emblem. It was made for Rolls-Royce by Charles Sykes, an eminent artist and sculptor, at the suggestion of the second Lord Montagu. Lord Montagu's secretary was Sykes' model.

The Car for the Rich Young Man

Ferdinand Porsche (1875–1952) was one of the finest automobile designers. Many people called him an artist, although he could not draw a straight line. He had the ability to communicate with his draftsmen, however, so that they could put exactly what he was thinking on paper. His designs broke new ground. Other car makers were in awe of the cars he produced and copied many of his original ideas.

On Display

It is difficult to design cars for famous people. These people need to be visible to everyone, and yet they need to be protected from potential danger. The **Pope-mobile**, as it came to be called, was a Range Rover adaptation with a "viewing room" at the back. It proved to be popular, both with the public, who had a good view of the pontiff, and also with the Pope, who was protected from harm as well as from the weather.

Every now and then, a car comes along that grabs the public imagination. It may do so for a variety of reasons — its design, its engineering, even its notoriety. These are the cars people want to own or to see. When cars appear in motion pictures, they create an impression, especially when the car does something out of the ordinary. Herbie, the VW Beetle, had a mind of its own. The DeLorean took its owners *Back to the Future*. Genevieve, the old car that refused to give up, created worldwide interest in **veteran** and **vintage cars**. Some cars are admired as works of art, and some people have particularly beautiful cars in their homes as a form of three-dimensional art.

The Most Popular Car in the World

Although Porsche designed the Volkswagen Beetle, the British car industry rejected it as too ugly. With the "Bug," Volkswagen went on to sell more cars than any other manufacturer, outselling the previous record holder, the Model T Ford. The Beetle was popular with all ages, and, because it had an air-cooled engine, there was no need for antifreeze in winter.

A Farmer's Car

The Citroen company asked Pierre Boulanger to produce a car that could carry a farmer's wife and a pig in the back, as well as a basket of eggs that would not break even when the car was driven across a plowed field. The result was the Citroen 2CV, which has been compared to an umbrella with four wheels underneath. Andre Citroen (1878–1935) started life as a maker of gears. His most successful gears had teeth shaped like a chevron. The chevron became the emblem he put on the front of his cars, and it is still used today.

A Car Full of Gadgets

Films featuring James Bond have always used spectacular gadgets, and this car (*right*) is no exception. It started life as an Aston Martin DB5, but it was transformed by the addition of revolving license plates, machine guns in the front, oil spray at the back, a bullet-proof back plate, and, best of all, an ejecting passenger seat that sends the passenger through the roof.

A Status Symbol

The E-Type Jaguar was the cult car of the 1960s. It was a road car with the performance of a racing car. Beautiful to look at, but with very simple lines, it became a status symbol. Its top speed of 150 miles (241 km) per hour made it popular, as did its price, which was much less than other comparable makes. Its gas consumption made it expensive to run.

The Best

Ferrari is renowned for producing the world's best cars, and one of the most sought after is the 250 GTO. It was commonly known as the Ant Eater because of its nose. Many famous names have raced in this car, including Stirling Moss, Roy Salvadori, and John Surtees. Only forty of these cars were made between 1962 and 1964.

Chitty, Chitty, Bang! Bang!

This multipurpose car could travel on land, water, and in the air. Ian Fleming, creator of James Bond, wrote about it in a book. His story was based on a real racing car in England.

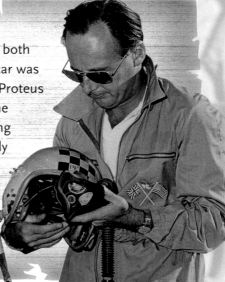

The Quest for Speed

Donald Campbell wanted to hold both land and water speed records. His car was called Bluebird and had a four-ton Bristol Proteus gas-turbine engine. His first attempt to break the record finished in disaster, with both the car and driver suffering badly. The car was rebuilt with a fin at the back to keep it steady at high speeds. In 1964, Donald Campbell broke the existing land record in Australia with a speed of 403.1 miles (649 km) per hour and the water speed record at 276 miles (444 km) per hour. Two years later, he tried to break his own record and was killed instantly when Bluebird crashed.

It always is difficult to predict the future. Will gasoline engines still be with us in fifty years? What other forms of power will be available? Will we even need personal transportation? The questions are many and varied. Alternative sources of power have been with us since the dawn of auto travel, but the difficulties of using them have kept them in the background. Already, we have instruments in the car to warn us of traffic jams ahead and to advise us on possible alternative routes. Will we be able to key our destination into a car's computer and then be whisked along by a linear motor with the technology under the road? Perhaps drivers of the future will have nothing to do except sit back and relax. Only time will tell.

Battery Power

This Ford car (*above*) uses electricity from a bank of batteries as power. It is very easy to drive and extremely quiet. It seems to be **pollution-free**, but the electricity needed to recharge the batteries is produced in power stations, which are great polluters.

Step on the Gas

Hyundai made an experimental engine (*below*) that runs on hydrogen gas, which seems to offer a good alternative to gasoline because it is inexpensive and easy to produce. Pollution would not be a problem, but storing the gas under pressure might be unsafe. **Hybrid** engines, which use either gasoline or electricity, seem to be a better option. Toyota, Honda, Lexus, Ford, Chevrolet, and GMC now produce hybrids.

Keeping Down Emissions

Concern over the environment has produced legislation all over the world to cut down on harmful **emissions** from automobiles caused by incomplete combustion of fuel and the addition of lead to keep the engine from "knocking." Advances in engine technology, the introduction of unleaded gasoline, and the use of catalytic converters — which are a kind of chemical filter — have improved the situation.

Straight from the Sun

This car is covered with **solar panels** that convert the Sun's energy into the electricity needed to drive the car. On the face of it, it seems an excellent form of transportation. The fuel is free, the car does not pollute, and it is easy to drive. There is always a down side. With current technology, the car needs to have a huge area covered with solar panels to get enough power from the Sun to run the car. This idea might work in Australia but not in Norway, where there are only a few hours of sunlight each day at certain times of the year.

Testing for Safety

Cars today probably are safer than they ever have been. They endure rigorous tests to see how effective they are in preventing injury to drivers and passengers. This photo shows a simulated head-on crash, in which a car is propelled into a wall. Front ends of cars now are built to crumple on impact and so absorb most of the shock. Side-impact tests determine the efficiency of special side-impact bars in the doors.

Faster Than Sound

The first land speed record was 39.24 miles (63 km) per hour, set by an electric car in 1898. Almost one hundred years later, Andy Green set the record at 763.035 miles (1,228 km) per hour in Thrust SSC in the Black Rock Desert of Nevada. In setting this record, Green broke the sound barrier, creating a sonic boom heard 15 miles (24 km) away.

The first car manufactured in the United States was a Winton. A Winton car also made the first coast-to-coast crossing of the United States in 1903. The trip took sixty-five days, but the driver spent twenty days repairing the car.

Many early cars had wooden bodies and leather mudguards. Curved boards in front of the driver's feet were also a feature of early cars, to stop dirt and stones being dashed into the car — the origin of the word "dashboard."

When automobile racing started, officials used flags to signal the drivers. In 1899, a red flag meant "stop," and a yellow flag meant "caution." Those two colors retain their meaning today.

In the early days of auto travel, people found starting their cars with a crank both difficult and dangerous. The introduction of the electric starter changed this situation. The first car with a standard electric starter was a Cadillac, in 1912.

The least-used, world-record-breaking car was the Golden Arrow. No one drove it until it arrived in Daytona in 1929. Henry Seagrave took it on one practice run and then set a new world land speed record of 231.44 miles (372.39 km) per hour. It has been driven only 20 miles (32 km).

The country producing the most cars before 1906 was France. After that, the United States took the lead. France continued to export the most cars until 1913.

Web Sites

About Inventors: Automobile History
inventors.about.com/library/inventors/blcar.htm
Find out details about famous automobiles and automobile inventors.

Who Invented the Automobile?
www.loc.gov/rr/scitech/mysteries/auto.html
Everyday Mysteries: Fun Science Facts from the Library of Congress

The Museum of Automobile History
www.themuseumofautomobilehistory.com/Gallery/index.html
Posters, paintings, and billboards of automobiles and automobile memorabilia.

accelerator — the pedal in a car that adds fuel to increase the rate of combustion and speed up the car

antifreeze — a substance added to a liquid to lower its freezing point

armor plated — covered with a protective metal outer layer

boiler — the part of a steam generator where water is converted into steam

brougham — a lightweight, closed. horse-drawn carriage with the driver outside in front

chassis — the supporting frame of an automobile

coat of arms — an emblem with a crest, the figures, and a motto that represents a particular family

containers — large, portable compartments, about the size of railroad cars, used for shipping freight

cylinder — the piston chamber in an engine

decarbonization — the act of removing the carbon from something

emissions — substances discharged into the air

four-stroke engine — an engine that has four movements of the piston before the entire engine firing sequence is repeated

front-wheel drive — a drive system in which only the front pair of wheels receives power from the engine

gear — a toothed wheel that turns a larger wheel

hood — the movable metal covering over the engine of an automobile

hood ornament — a small sculpture, representing a person, animal, or object placed on the front of a car to bring good luck

hybrid — a car that has two engines, one run by gasoline, the other by electricity or hydrogen gas

internal combustion engine — an engine in which the heat that generates the power is created inside the engine proper instead of within an external furnace

jack — a tool for lifting a car or another heavy object a short distance

methanol — a volatile, flammable liquid alcohol, used as antifreeze or mixed with other chemicals

patronage — the support or influence of a patron or protector

piston — a sliding piece moved by or moving against fluid pressure

pneumatic tire — a tire that is inflated with compressed air

pollution-free — free of contamination from harmful wastes, especially of extra carbon dioxide

Pope-mobile — an automobile with a passenger wagon encased in glass so that observers can see the celebrity and the celebrity will be safe from harm

production line — a line of work stations designed for efficiency

radiator — a device for transferring heat from the fluid within to an area or object outside

robotic arm — a machine that performs complicated, often repetitive, tasks in place of a human being

running board — a footboard at the side of an automobile

solar panels — batteries that use radiant energy from the Sun as a power source

spark plug — a part in an engine that throws a spark to make the engine start

suspension — the system that lets a car's wheels move over bumps, while the rider stays steady

valve — a mechanical device that starts or stops the flow of a liquid or a gas

veteran car — a car built before January 1905

vintage car — a car of old, recognized, and enduring interest, importance, or quality

water jacket — the enclosed space surrounding the cylinder block of an internal combustion engine

windshield — a transparent screen that protects the occupants of a car from wind and weather